GEMS NATURE'S JEWELS

AMETHYSTS

By Emily Jankowski Mahoney

Gareth Stevens PUBLISHING

Please visit our website, www.garethstevens.com. For a free color catalog of all our high-quality books, call toll free 1-800-542-2595 or fax 1-877-542-2596.

Library of Congress Cataloging-in-Publication Data

Mahoney, Emily Jankowski, author.
Amethysts / Emily Jankowski Mahoney.
pages cm. — (Gems : nature's jewels)
Includes bibliographical references and index.
ISBN 978-1-4824-2856-8 (pbk.)
ISBN 978-1-4824-2857-5 (6 pack)
ISBN 978-1-4824-2858-2 (library binding)
1. Amethysts—Juvenile literature. 2. Precious stones—Juvenile literature. I. Title.
QE394.A4M34 2016
553.8'7—dc23
2014049862

First Edition

Published in 2016 by
Gareth Stevens Publishing
111 East 14th Street, Suite 349
New York, NY 10003

Designer: Andrea Davison-Bartolotta
Editor: Kristen Rajczak

Photo credits: Cover, p. 1 Sergieiev/Shutterstock.com; p. 5 (main) Miriam Doerr/Shutterstock.com; p. 5 (inset) J. Palys/Shutterstock.com; p. 7 Frans Lemmens/Getty Images; p. 8 Imfoto/Shutterstock.com; p. 9 kritskaya/Shutterstock.com; p. 11 (left) © iStockphoto.com/VYG; p. 11 (right) © iStockphoto.com/PhilipCacka; p. 13 (both) Dennis Macdonald/Getty Images; p. 15 Marie-Lan Nguyen/Wikimedia Commons; p. 16 Chursina Viktoriia/Shutterstock.com; p. 17 JoeFotoSS/Shutterstock.com; p. 18 TaraPatta/Shutterstock.com; p. 19 ekler/Shutterstock.com; p. 20 DEA/G. Dagli Orti/Getty Images; p. 21 Vangert/Shutterstock.com.

Printed in the United States of America

CPSIA compliance information: Batch #CS15GS: For further information contact Gareth Stevens, New York, New York at 1-800-542-2595.

Contents

Words in the glossary appear in **bold** type the first time they are used in the text.

Amazing Amethysts

Amethysts are beautiful purple gems that belong to the **quartz** family. In fact, amethysts are the most **valuable** kind of quartz!

Amethysts can be different shades of purple, including those with hints of blue or red. The most valuable color is a very deep purple. This gem is especially popular for **jewelry** because it's very hard and **durable**. People have been using amethysts for jewelry since the time of the ancient Greeks and Romans. Back then, amethyst was believed to have magical properties!

Be a Gem Genius!

Minerals are matter in the ground that forms rocks. Gems are stones that are cut and **polished** and are worth money. They're often the crystals some minerals form in rock.

Amethysts are popular, beautiful gems.

Where Are Amethysts Found?

Amethysts can be found all over the world, but they're most common in South America, especially in Brazil and Uruguay, as well as in Madagascar. Amethysts from different places have different colors. Those from Brazil are lighter purple, while amethysts from Madagascar are reddish in color. Amethysts are often found in Germany and near the Ural Mountains in Russia, too.

There are amethyst **deposits** in the United States, although the gems found in them commonly aren't of high enough **quality** to set in jewelry.

Be a Gem Genius!

Amethysts are a purple color because of the iron in their crystal structure. Some scientists think the element manganese may play a part in the color, too.

This amethyst was found in the country of Morocco in northern Africa.

Making an Amethyst

When they're first found, amethysts are commonly short and have a shape like a **pyramid**. However, some of these gems from Mexico are quite long and are a mix of purples.

Amethysts are found mostly in **igneous rock**. Hot liquid rock from deep within Earth rises to the surface as lava, forming **cavities** and cracks as it goes. When the right mix of the elements silica and iron is present, amethyst crystals grow in these open spaces inside the rock.

Be a Gem Genius!

When amethysts are heated, they form a kind of gem called citrine, which is orange yellow in color.

citrine ▶

Amethysts have many sides, or facets, even before they're cut into jewelry.

Geodes

Geodes are hollow rocks lined with gems such as amethysts. Geodes form when gas bubbles in cooling lava leave behind cavities. Water containing minerals later fills the cavity. When enough minerals build up, gems form inside the geode. Geodes can weigh several tons and be 10 feet (3 m) tall!

People can create amethysts, too! They were first made in labs for use in electronics, or things powered by electricity. It's very hard to tell man-made amethysts from natural amethysts.

Be a Gem Genius!

Lab-created quartz can be used to make parts of computers, TVs, and cell phones!

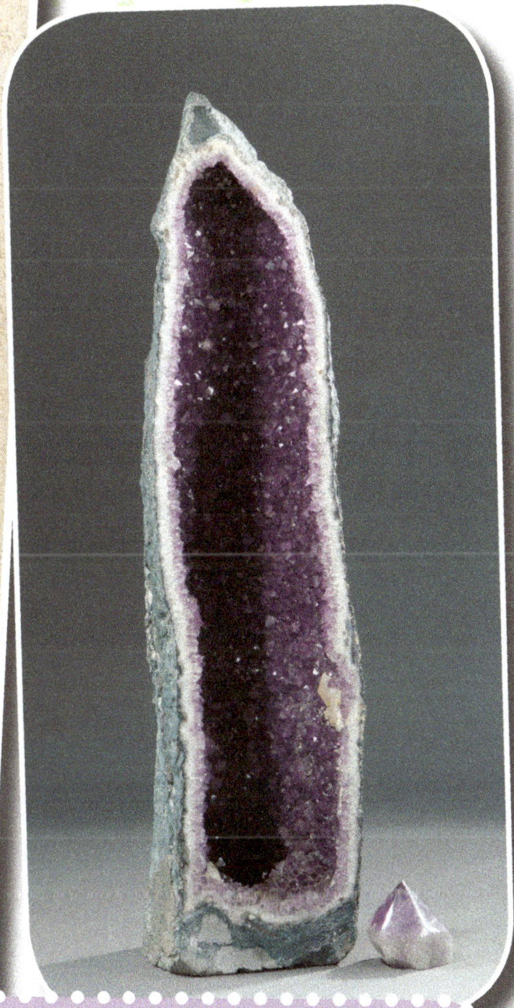

Geodes can be many shapes, including long tubelike shapes like the geodes shown here.

Find a Gem!

Like many gems, amethysts are mined. Amethyst miners often use the drift mining method to find gems. They don't dig *down* to find amethysts. Instead, a tunnel, or drift, is made into the side of a mountain.

Amethyst Mine Panorama is the largest known amethyst deposit in North America. Found in Canada near Thunder Bay, Ontario, the mine was discovered when workers were building a road. At Amethyst Mine Panorama, visitors can dig for their own amethysts to take home!

Be a Gem Genius!

The color of some amethysts will fade if left in sunlight too long.

Visitors to the Amethyst Mine Panorama can see amethyst cut into jewelry, too.

What Makes Amethysts Valuable?

In general, the deeper color purple the amethyst is, the more valuable it is. Reddish purple amethysts are more prized than just dark purple. How clear the gem is, or its clarity, is also part of an amethyst's worth. If the gem contains many inclusions, or imperfections, it isn't considered to be as valuable.

Finally, the size of the amethyst is very important. Larger stones are almost always more valuable than smaller ones, unless they have many inclusions.

Be a Gem Genius!

Gems are measured using a unit called a carat. One carat is equal to 0.007 ounce (200 mg).

Gems can be valuable because of their age or use as art, too. This portrait, carved into amethyst, dates back nearly 2,000 years!

Making Amethyst Jewelry

In order to make amethysts into beautiful jewelry, the gems must be cleaned, smoothed, and shaped. Only then are they made to fit into rings, earrings, and more.

Amethysts are very hard. That means an even harder mineral must be used to cut them. Lapidaries, or those who cut and shape gems out of raw crystals, use a saw made of diamond! The gems must be cut slowly and carefully so the crystal **structure** is unharmed.

Be a Gem Genius!

On the Mohs scale of mineral hardness, amethysts are a 7 out of 10. Diamonds are a 10, the hardest mineral.

Lapidaries cut the gems they're working with in a way that will cause them to catch the most light and, as a result, sparkle more.

Famous Amethysts

The largest amethyst geode ever found weighs 2.5 tons (2.27 mt) and is called the Empress of Uruguay, named after the country where it was found. In 2011, someone broke off and stole a tennis ball-sized piece!

One of the most famous pieces of amethyst jewelry belonged to Queen Charlotte of England. The bracelet was said to be worth thousands of dollars at the beginning of the eighteenth century. Years later, it was much less valuable because more amethyst deposits had been found.

Amethyst was considered a rare and valuable stone until large deposits were found in Africa, Brazil, and Mexico. This map shows amethyst deposits in Brazil.

Amethyst in History

Amethyst is one of the oldest recorded gemstones. Many ancient Egyptian tombs, dating back thousands of years, had jewelry with amethyst. The ancient Greeks believed their god Dionysus created the gem. Amethyst was also used in churches during the **Middle Ages**, and church leaders called bishops wore amethyst rings.

Today, amethysts are common, especially for those born in February. It's the birthstone for that month! You can also see their beautiful geodes on display in many museums.

ancient Egyptian amethyst jewelry

Forming Amethyst Geodes

Glossary

cavity: a hole or an empty space inside a solid thing

deposit: an amount of a mineral in the ground that built up over a period of time

durable: able to withstand wear and harm

igneous rock: solid rock that was once the hot, liquid rock found deep within Earth

jewelry: pieces of metal, often holding gems, worn on the body

Middle Ages: a time in European history from about 500 to about 1500

polish: to make smooth and shiny

pyramid: a 3-D shape that has a rectangular base and triangular sides

quality: the standard or grade of something

quartz: a mineral that often grows colorless crystals, but can also be colored

structure: the way something is arranged

valuable: worth a lot of money

For More Information

Books

Petersen, Christine. *Groovy Gems.* Edina, MN: ABDO Publishing, 2010.

Symes, R. F., and R. R. Harding. *Crystal & Gem.* New York, NY: DK Publishing, 2014.

Tomecek, Steve. *Everything Rocks and Minerals.* Washington, DC: National Geographic, 2010.

Websites

The Dynamic Earth
www.mnh.si.edu/earth/text/
Explore gems, minerals, and mining at the National Museum of Natural History website.

The Mineral and Gemstone Kingdom
www.minerals.net
Read about gems and minerals.

Index